Skinwalker Ranch

Facing the Unknown Force that Haunts the Uinta Basin

Conrad Bauer

Copyrights

All rights reserved © 2018 by Conrad Bauer and Maplewood Publishing. No part of this publication or the information in it may be quoted from or reproduced in any form by means such as printing, scanning, photocopying, or otherwise without prior written permission of the copyright holder.

Disclaimer and Terms of Use

Efforts has been made to ensure that the information in this book is accurate and complete. However, the author and the publisher do not warrant the accuracy of the information, text, and graphics contained within the book due to the rapidly changing nature of science, research, known and unknown facts, and internet. The author and the publisher do not hold any responsibility for errors, omissions, or contrary interpretation of the subject matter herein. This book is presented solely for motivational and informational purposes only

ISBN: 978-1720423836

Printed in the United States

Contents

The Skinwalker and the Conspiracy of Silence _____ 1

The Beginning of a Mystery _____ 3

The Shermans meet the Skin-Walkers _____ 7

Flying Refrigerators and Mysterious Mind Games _____ 11

Closer Encounters _____ 17

Yes, They're Watching Us _____ 23

Last Stand at the Ranch House _____ 27

How Robert Bigelow Bought the Farm _____ 31

Higher Dimensions _____ 37

Skin-Walkers and Vandals _____ 43

Further Developments _____ 49

Possible Explanations _____ 53

More Questions than Answers _____ 73

Further Readings _____ 75

Also by Conrad Bauer _____ 79

The Skinwalker and the Conspiracy of Silence

The world is full of mystifying myths and legends, but the Navajo legend of the skin-walker is one of the least understood of all. Indeed, it is perhaps the only mythological entity whose originators seem to be sworn to complete secrecy on the subject. Most Navajo are hesitant even to mention skin-walkers in passing conversation among themselves, and if an outsider were to ask about these mythical creatures, he would receive nothing but a startled and stone-faced denial.

But the walls of silence that have been built up around the skin-walker are not airtight. A few obscure, anecdotal stories of shape-shifting entities playing pranks on the locals have found their way through the embargo. From them we have learned that the skin-walker of hushed Native American legend has a name in Navajo that is never supposed to be pronounced, or even mentioned. But if you feel brave enough to sound it out in your own mind—the Navajo name for these fearsome fiends is "naaldooshii".

According to Navajo folklore, the mere utterance of this name is dangerous because it could draw the unwanted attention of a skin-walker. As scary as these entities are, the myth maintains that skin-walkers were originally human beings. Specifically, they were medicine men or shamans who achieved superhuman awareness and mastery of their soul but turned toward the darker side of reality somewhere along their spiritual journey. For some unknown reason, these once-holy men, after reaching enlightenment, simply chose to become evil.

This induction into the negative side of the universe came with an initiation. In order for a skin-walker to obtain his extraordinary powers, he had to kill someone of his own bloodline. This previously holy man was then imbued with the sinister and unholy power of the skin-walker, which included the ability to shape-shift into just about any animal known to man—and some that were completely unknown outside of legend.

The most infamous of these animal forms is that of a highly unusual dog/wolf/coyote type creature that is usually much larger than its natural counterpart. These strange canines can run at incredible, unheard-of speed, and they have even been witnessed running on two legs.

As if these canine aberrations weren't frightening enough, the skin-walker is also connected to a more primatal strain of the paranormal. Many have witnessed these shape-shifters morph into furry, ape-like creatures. These entities can only be described as the classic Bigfoot or Sasquatch of North American folklore.

And this is only the tip of the paranormal iceberg. As we proceed with the true story of the skin-walkers and the Utah ranch that became infamous for hosting them, we will break the conspiracy of silence that has long surrounded the skin-walker wide open.

The Beginning of a Mystery

Most stories have a clear beginning and a clear end, but the beginning of the great mystery that is Skinwalker Ranch and its immediate surroundings could be as old as the beginning of time. Native Americans have passed around legends about this haunted corner of Utah long before the ranch or any other permanent settlement existed. But the European settlers who came after them would note the high strangeness as well, and perhaps that's a good place for us to start the tale.

Mormon leader Brigham Young was one of the earlier chroniclers of this Utah oddity. Young succeeded the founder of the Mormon faith, Joseph Smith, as president of the Church of Jesus Christ of Latter-day Saints after Smith's assassination. He then led his followers west to escape further religious persecution, establishing several Mormon colonies in what was then unsettled American territory. One of these colonies was located on what would one day become the grounds of Skinwalker Ranch.

Brigham Young's first forays into this haunted stretch of land occurred in the early 1860s when he sent a survey team to see if the Uinta Basin would provide habitable land for settlers. Their findings were disappointing; when they came back, they reported that the whole region was a "vast contiguity of waste" which was completely "valueless except for nomadic purposes, hunting grounds for Indians and to hold the world together".

Despite this bleak early assessment, the Mormon march eventually did bring the Church of Latter-day Saints back to the Uinta Basin, with serious settlement effort occurring in the 1880s. Upon venturing into this formerly Native American land, the Mormons soon had many of their own skin-walker tales to tell. The secret mythology was secret no longer, and the tales then spread to miners who arrived around 1885 to harvest the Uinta Basin's many valuable mineral deposits.

The surrounding area, named Uintah County, now boasts a population of some 25,000 people. It is thus still sparsely populated by most standards, but considering the vastness of the region, which those first Mormon explorers quantified as "valueless except for nomadic purposes", the figure demonstrates slow but steady growth. Today the miners are all but gone, and cattle ranching has been the Uinta Basin's main industry since the early 1950s—which is also when the first documented UFO sightings began to take place over the area.

Junior Hicks, a science professor at the University of Utah, was the first to gather evidence of the paranormal happenings at Skinwalker Ranch and attempt to figure out what was going on. Hicks's investigation was inspired by a group of students who witnessed what could only be described as a UFO over

Skinwalker Ranch in 1951. About 30 of his students claimed to have seen a classic cigar-shaped UFO flying over them in broad daylight.

They had no doubt that they had observed something highly extraordinary, and it turned out that they weren't the only ones. Hicks's subsequent digging uncovered hundreds of firsthand accounts of UFOs and other strange phenomena occurring in and around the ranch. He soon discovered that all of these tales shared one common feature—and that common feature was the skin-walker. Hicks was one of the first outsiders to collect extensive information about these alleged paranormal entities from Native American tribes.

The tribal members he spoke with referred to the whole region as the "Path of the Skin-Walker" and were steadfast in their refusal to go anywhere near it. Hicks eventually published his findings in a 1974 book entitled *The Utah UFO Display*—the first book in which skin-walkers were directly linked to the UFO phenomenon. Although Hicks mentioned the Skinwalker Ranch in this book, the ranch itself did not attract much attention until the early 1990s when the Sherman family bought the land and brought the phenomena that came with it to the world stage.

The Shermans, undoubtedly the most famous residents of Skinwalker Ranch, acquired it after the deaths of the original owners, Kenneth John Myers and Edith Child Myers. This married couple had purchased the ranch all the way back in 1933. At first their property consisted of just 160 acres, but over the years they expanded their holdings to 480 acres. They never had any children, instead throwing themselves completely into working the land.

Even after Kenneth passed away in 1987, Edith stayed on at the ranch by herself until her own death on March 3, 1994.

Kenneth's younger brother Garth Myers inherited the property and eventually sold it to Terry and Gwen Sherman. Not a whole lot is known about what went on before the Shermans moved in, but when they did they were absolutely puzzled to find locks and deadbolts all throughout the ranch house.

There were locks on both the insides and outsides of doors, windows, and even closets. Were the previous residents really afraid of unwelcome visitors suddenly invading their closet space? Most of us believe the monster in the closet is just a product of vivid childhood imagination, but here was a home with no children, whose inhabitants were seemingly afraid of what might lurk in their bedroom closet! It all begged the question—just what had the Myers family been trying so desperately to keep out?

The Shermans Meet the Skin-Walkers

When the Sherman family purchased the old Myers Ranch, they assumed that they would be the only ones living on the premises. But soon enough, they began to realize that they had some company on the land. The first of these strange denizens made its presence known in the classic skin-walker form—as an oddly out-of-place wolf.

Terry Sherman had been hard at work in one of the fields surrounding the ranch house when he saw movement out of the corner of his eye. He turned to see some kind of large dog-like creature in the distance. It was walking in his direction, and he immediately began a process of elimination to figure out what it might be—a dog, a coyote, or perhaps even a wolf. As it came closer, however, Terry was forced to discard such easy explanations. Whatever it was, this creature was bigger than any natural-born canine had any right to be.

Before he knew what was happening, the wolfish creature had covered the entire distance between them and trotted right out in front of Terry and his family. The animal seemed peaceful, maybe even tame, and Terry couldn't help but reach out his hand to pet it. He ran his hand through its grey fur, feeling the powerful musculature below. But this animal would not remain friendly for long.

Shortly after Terry touched it, the beast turned around and ran away from him, shooting off like a thunderbolt and heading straight toward the corral in which the Shermans kept their cattle. Before Terry knew quite what was happening, it stuck its snout through the bars of the cattle pen and clamped its jaws onto the head of the calf closest to it. Taking a vise-grip with its teeth, the creature began attempting to pull the baby bovine through the bars as it screamed in pain.

Terry was shocked at what he was seeing, but he finally got over his surprise and ran to help the calf. Reaching the side of the wolf—or whatever it was—he delivered several blows to the beast's ribcage. When his bare hands had no effect, Terry upped the ante by grabbing a nearby baseball bat which he sent crashing down onto the attacking animal's side and back.

But incredibly, the wolf-creature still seemed completely unaffected. Ignoring Terry altogether, it continued its attempt to pull the crying calf through the bars of its holding pen. Desperate to stop this shameless seizure of his livestock, Terry yelled out to his son Tad, "Get my magnum!" He meant the heavy-duty handgun that he kept in his pickup truck. Tad quickly brought the weapon to his father, and Terry opened fire, scoring several direct hits on the wolf-thing.

Strangely, even after being riddled with bullets, the beast didn't deign to acknowledge that it was being shot! And what startled Terry even more was that his blasts left no visible bullet wounds or blood. The wolfish interloper seemed completely impervious to the gunshot onslaught. It wasn't until the fourth shot, at point-blank range, that the creature finally let go of the calf—seemingly more out of sheer annoyance than anything else.

The freed baby cow ran to the safety of the other side of the corral, still wailing in pain and fear and bleeding from its injuries. Terry was left alone just a few feet from the wolf-thing, and to his amazement, it still seemed completely unharmed as it stared blankly back at him. Beginning to break into an all-out panic, Terry aimed his gun at the creature's chest and let loose with one more magnum round. He made a direct hit, but the animal's only response was to slowly turn around and begin walking away at a leisurely pace.

If the wolf-thing had been injured by the barrage of bullets, it didn't show it. Becoming increasingly concerned, and not willing to allow such a dangerous animal to live to raid his livestock again, Terry yelled for his son to bring him his shotgun. Armed with this much more powerful weapon, Terry opened fire on the creature once again. This time the sound of impact could be heard clearly as the 12-gauge slug tore through the animal's shoulder.

Even now the creature made only the briefest of reactions, pausing for just a moment before continuing at its own slowly measured pace. Terry, shocked and somewhat incensed at the sight, then let off another round, hitting the wolf-thing directly in the chest. This time Terry could clearly see gouts of blood spraying out of the open wound, but even so, the animal didn't show itself to be in any pain whatsoever as it slowly continued its course toward a patch of trees.

Terry and his son were still desperate to stop the beast. They followed it into the woods, but lost sight of it after it entered the trees. However, they could clearly see its fresh tracks in the mud, and they carefully followed them—right up until the trail suddenly reached a dead-end in the middle of the forest. With no explanation whatsoever, the tracks simply stopped. Their werewolf visitor had apparently disappeared in mid-gallop.

The incident was deeply disturbing for the Shermans, but as they would soon find out, this kind of bizarre cat-and-mouse, smoke-and-mirrors deviltry was standard fare for the intruding tricksters that they would come to know all too well during their stay on the Skinwalker Ranch. This was the Sherman family's first run-in with what they would come to know as a skin-walker—but it wouldn't be their last.

Flying Refrigerators and Mysterious Mind Games

As the Sherman family tried their best to put the unsettling encounter with the "bullet-proof wolf" behind them, they gained some small sense of solace when they learned from longtime local residents that unusually big wolves weren't all that uncommon in the area. Of course, this still didn't explain how the animal had survived several shotgun blasts, but information allowed the Shermans to rationalize the incident. Perhaps Terry simply hadn't hit any vital organs. They put the whole thing out of their minds.

The mysterious wolf-thing, however, wasn't so willing to let bygones be bygones. It soon showed up again, following Gwen's car as she drove up to the ranch house—and moving at such an uncanny speed that it was easily able to keep up with the vehicle before finally going on its way. Gwen, realizing that this was the same exact creature reported by her husband Terry, decided that enough was enough and made up her mind to complain about the intruding animal.

This meant a visit to the Office of Tribal Affairs located in nearby Fort Duchesne, where she related a sanitized version of the "bullet-proof wolf" incident as well as her own wolf sighting. Gwen was a no-nonsense woman and she expected to get results, but all she received from the local magistrates was a look of bewilderment. Despite what the Shermans had heard from their neighbors, the tribal officials informed her that there had not been a wolf in the region for many decades; they had been wiped out in 1929! Sidestepping the wolf-thing's unnatural speed and seeming invulnerability, the officials insisted that it was an utter impossibility for the Shermans to have seen a wolf at all, suggesting that it must have been a stray dog or coyote instead.

After this rebuff Gwen returned home more anxious, confused and frustrated than ever. What was it that they had seen? Were their eyes simply playing tricks on them?

If that was the case, Terry was the next Sherman to be subject to a massive hallucination. The incident began innocently enough, when Terry, his son, and his nephew were out surveying the property right around sunset. As the skies began to darken around them, Terry noticed what looked like the headlights of a parked RV in the distance. It certainly wasn't unheard of for an RV to park on someone else's ranch—this sort of thing happens all the time in the vast expanse of the Utah countryside. But that didn't mean Terry liked it, and he wasn't about to tolerate such trespassers on his property.

Determined to order the interlopers off his land, he instructed his son and nephew to follow him as he walked in the direction of the lights. But almost as soon as they began heading in the RV's direction, it began to back away from them. This seemed strange to Terry, since they were still too far away to be seen against the dim backdrop. Maybe, he thought, the trespassers had a pair of binoculars or night-vision goggles trained on them and were watching their every movement.

The notion of being spied on—and on his own property, no less—only incensed Terry further, so the three broke into a run and began to give chase to what they still believed to be a departing RV. But as they drew closer, they were stunned to see the vehicle's headlights lift off the ground and then land a few feet away. Terry wasn't sure what was happening. Had the RV hit a piece of uneven terrain and been jolted into the air? He wasn't exactly sure—but he knew that the vehicle was now approaching a grove of olive trees lined with a barbed wire fence.

Terry thought that they had the RV cornered. Intent on confronting the interlopers, he broke into a full sprint. As they closed with the vehicle, Terry began to realize just how strange this supposed RV really was. It was moving, but it wasn't making any sound—no engine noise, no sound of tires rolling across the ground, nothing. Things got even stranger as the craft neared the fence-lined trees. This would have constituted a dead end for a real RV, but Terry and the boys watched in shock as the vehicle lifted off the ground and silently hovered for a moment before flying right over the tops of the trees! They were now able to make out the object more clearly, and strangely enough it looked like an oversized refrigerator, with one light shining in front and a red beacon shining in back.

They were all astounded, and Terry's nephew was so shocked that he would never return to the ranch again. Just like the "bullet-proof wolf", though, the "flying refrigerator" couldn't seem to stay away. In fact, the odd object returned in only a few short weeks. This time Terry was out walking with his wife Gwen when they suddenly heard a loud metallic scraping sound. They turned and once again saw what appeared to be headlights.

Not sure what to make of it, and wondering if perhaps someone was lost on their property, they began to walk toward the lights. As soon as they neared the object, however, it lifted off the ground and flew a few feet further away. With a sinking feeling, Terry realized that this was no ordinary motorist—it was the same hopping vehicle he had seen before. He and Gwen continued to walk toward the craft, and it continued to rise and move further away as they approached.

As the bizarre refrigerator-shaped object seemingly played cat-and-mouse with them, Terry actually began to grow angry. As strange as the whole situation was, he felt as if whatever was behind it was playing games with them. For what purpose, he couldn't imagine—but playing games nonetheless. Trying to overcome his fear with righteous anger, Terry shouted, "Who the hell do they think they are?" Just after this indignant inquiry, they heard the loud scraping sound again—this time directly to their rear. They turned to see what was causing the noise, but saw nothing—and when they turned back to the refrigerator-shaped object, it was gone.

This is certainly an odd account, but it does have one aspect that just might have a rational explanation. That aspect is the shape of the object. According to Terry, the vehicle looked like a "flying refrigerator". Well, interestingly enough, the top-secret aircraft test facility in nearby Nevada, Area 51, at one time produced an aircraft that seems to fit this description.

The now-declassified aircraft called the Tacit Blue was indeed widely described as resembling a "flying refrigerator". This very strange looking craft had an extremely unorthodox box-shaped body designed to make it invisible to radar. Tacit Blue utilized a far different approach toward radar deflection than the now-familiar diamond shapes of the F117 and Stealth Bomber. It was basically a flying box—or refrigerator!

Could this possibly have been the vehicle that Terry and Gwen witnessed performing maneuvers on their ranch? Was it the Tacit Blue on a test flight? But even if it was the Tacit Blue—which was still very much top secret in 1994 when the Shermans claim to have seen it—that still doesn't quite explain the odd cat-and-mouse behavior of the craft. Nor can it account for the bizarre metallic sounds projected away from the vehicle.

It seemed to the Shermans almost as if the object had used the loud metallic noise to get their attention, and then used the same projected sound to distract them so it could disappear. Of course, this gives no hint as to what the craft was or who was in it—but it certainly seems to show they were in the mood for mind games!

Closer Encounters

After the family's strange encounters with the refrigerator-shaped craft, Terry began to believe that someone was using their property for tests and exercises of a nature he could only imagine. From time to time, he contemplated the strange thought that perhaps his land was being used by some secret, black budget program of the United States government to test out exotic new technology.

As the wintertime months got underway, the strange phenomena that continued to beset his homestead furthered his speculation. One incident in particular that seemed to lend credence to the military black budget theory came when Terry was out checking on his cattle in the snowy fields. Suddenly—as almost always seems to be the case with this odd phenomenon—he detected movement out of the corner of his eye.

Turning to see what it was, he saw what looked like some sort of variation of the B-2 Stealth Bomber hovering over the snow just a few yards away. The B-2 Bomber had already been declassified and officially introduced to the American public a few years before, but even though Terry had this vague point of reference linking the craft to something plausible, explainable, and terrestrial, one can only imagine how strange it would be to have such an exotic aircraft drop down on his property!

Making the intrusion even stranger was the odd stillness that permeated the atmosphere surrounding the craft. There was no sound, no engine noise, nothing—just absolute and uncanny quiet as the vehicle hovered in place. This is not a known characteristic of any terrestrial craft. As advanced as the B-2 might be by earthly standards, it makes noise. The B-2 is considered stealthy because it can evade radar as it flies high up in the clouds, but it's nowhere near stealthy enough to hover a few feet off the ground in perfect silence!

Terry continued to watch as the gravity-defying object slowly drifted over the ground. As it came a little closer he noticed that it was emitting a colorful searchlight from the bottom of its hull, sending down a series of odd rainbow hues to illuminate the snowy ground below. Terry got the distinct impression that the craft was scanning the ground and searching for something.

Interestingly enough, the Uinta Basin of which the Skinwalker Ranch is a part is fabulously rich in rare mineral deposits. In fact, one such mineral discovered in the late 1880s, gilsonite, is one of the rarest of the so-called "black hydrocarbons", and the Uinta Basin contains one of the few major deposits of gilsonite on the planet. Was this craft—wherever it came from, and whoever it belonged to—conducting covert missions on the Shermans' property to retrieve this precious mineral?

In complete bewilderment, Terry decided that all he could do was watch. Sitting down on the snowy ridge, he attempted to make sense of the scene before him. The craft continued to trace the snow with colorful pinpoints of illumination that Terry would later refer to as "disco lights". The craft sent these strange, intrusive spotlights from one stretch of ground to another in a seemingly purposeful fashion, as if conducting a dogged search.

Terry was craning his neck to keep the craft in view as it passed nearby when his cervical vertebrae popped. Unexpectedly, this ordinarily trivial event had an immediate impact on the hovering craft. As soon as the bones in Terry's neck popped, ever so subtly breaking the silence of the snowy waste, the craft turned off all of its lighting. It had apparently detected the faint sound of human vertebrae popping from several yards away and learned of the presence of its quiet observer—Terry Sherman. For a moment, fear gripped Terry's heart as he began to imagine the sinister-looking ship attacking him, but to his immense relief the craft slowly moved away instead. He didn't know what to make of the sighting, but as is often the case with such unusual phenomenon, Terry found himself simultaneously repulsed and fascinated by the enigmatic activity.

Once again, Gwen had her own encounter with a "visitor" first seen by Terry when she was driving back to the ranch house one night a few weeks later. Looking up to admire what appeared to be a dark black cloud overhead, she realized that the "cloud" was actually the same strange craft that Terry had witnessed. But instead of being indifferent or wary, as it had been towards Terry, the craft seemed intent on following her. Gwen became increasingly uneasy as she made her way back to the ranch house. Finally unable to tolerate the pursuit anymore, she hit the gas pedal to try to get away from the craft. As soon as she did, it showered her with the same odd, colorful spotlight Terry had seen it illuminate the ground with. The lights followed her all the way to the driveway, and Gwen wondered in terror whether the craft would stop, or perhaps even land, when she parked her car. Fortunately for her frayed nerves, the ship simply continued on its way, flying over the house and disappearing over the horizon.

But Gwen's night of high strangeness wasn't over yet. Just an hour later, after she had settled into the house and called Terry (who was away on business that night), she spotted what looked like an RV on her property. She was both irked and somewhat alarmed that someone would have the gall to set up camp on their land.

Looking closer, she saw that the RV's interior was brightly illuminated. She could clearly see a desk through the vehicle's side windows—and she was then startled to see a figure dressed all in black stride into view, pull up a seat and sit down at the desk. As she strained her eyes to make out the details, she was perplexed to notice that the figure was wearing a helmet and some kind of uniform.

Was this person from the military? Why was he casually sitting down at his desk in the middle of the Shermans' ranch? Gwen was still asking herself these questions when the figure suddenly stood up and marched to the door of the RV. As she peered out at him, she realized that he was unusually tall, perhaps even seven feet. She could also now make out the details of his uniform. He had a black visor covering most of his face and knee-high boots on his feet.

She also noticed something troubling—the entity, who or what ever it was, appeared to be looking right at her. Perhaps the visor was a pair of long-distance night vision goggles, because Gwen had the distinct feeling that even from the considerable distance between them, the being was able to watch her every move. The same terror she had experienced earlier in the evening with the sighting of the unknown aircraft returned anew with this latest apparition. Gwen quickly averted her gaze and closed her curtains, then frantically dialed her husband and asked him to come home as soon as possible. Terry raced back to the ranch, but the supposed "RV" was long gone when he finally arrived.

Although Gwen did not see this particular object rise up into the air, its general description is very similar to the "flying refrigerator" that Terry had spotted several weeks earlier. Terry had initially thought that that interloper was an RV as well—that is, until it began to levitate! Whatever it was that Terry had seen, perhaps Gwen was seeing the same exact thing.

However, in Gwen's case, she actually saw one of the craft's occupants. And from the way the being stared at her through vision enhancing headgear, it appeared that even as the Shermans observed the strange phenomena of the Skinwalker Ranch, they too were being actively monitored and watched.

Yes, They're Watching Us

Even before the beginning of the UFO phenomenon, it has been speculated that humanity is being observed by another sentient species. All the way back in 1898, H.G. Wells opened his famous science fiction classic *War of the Worlds* with the line, "No one would have believed in the last years of the nineteenth century that this world was being watched keenly and closely by intelligences greater than man's and yet as mortal as his own."

Wells envisioned a Martian civilization spying on the Earth of the late 1800s with no one the wiser—but could an alien force really be sending out scouts and probes to observe humanity in its natural habitat? Humans, after all, have already sent robotic probes to most of the worlds in our solar system, so it may not be too farfetched to suppose that if aliens exist, they've sent some probes of their own.

In fact, one of the big questions for scientists searching for extraterrestrial life is, "Where are the probes?" According to the late great Stephen Hawking, if advanced aliens ever existed at any time during the history of our 13-billion-year-old universe, we should have bumped into one of their mechanical probes by now. Even if the aliens themselves went extinct billions of years ago, their robotic probes—just like the hundreds of autonomous craft humanity has launched into space—should still be out there.

Officially, at least, no scientist or NASA astronaut has ever bumped into any alien probes. But maybe they've been looking in the wrong place—because according to the Shermans, if you stick around Skinwalker Ranch long enough some very strange pieces of equipment of an unknown intelligence will undoubtedly make their appearance. They come in the form of lighted mechanical balls that seem to completely defy gravity.

Terry and Gwen first encountered these odd orbs one evening as they were out checking on their cattle. They noticed that their animals were unusually restless, and soon they too began to feel uneasy. The Shermans began to experience that strange but undeniable feeling that someone—or something—was watching them. Their horses were grazing under a nearby tree, and when Terry happened to look over at them, he was startled to see what appeared to be a perfectly round glass ball floating above the tree. Blue light was emanating from its crystalline surface.

Gwen turned to see what her husband was looking at and gasped in shock as the blue, baseball-sized light drifted away from the tree and slowly sailed down to one of the horses. As the pulsating blue orb hovered around the animal's head, it grew understandably agitated and stopped grazing. The object almost seemed to be filming the horse, or gathering some other kind of data, as it bathed the beast in an incredibly intense blue light.

Stunned as he was, Terry was also worried about what the unknown object might do to his horse. He felt compelled to take some sort of decisive action, but before he could move a muscle to intercept the object, it abruptly rose up and shot off away from the horse. To the Shermans' amazement, it then flew right over their heads, about 20 feet above them. As the couple stared in shock, the object just hovered silently, fixed in that position, as if it were watching them intently.

From this distance they could see that the object was made of crystal-clear glass and was about the size of a softball or a small melon. Some blue liquid bubbled and swirled inside. Terry could also hear a slight crackling being emitted from the strange probe; it reminded him of static electricity. As the couple stared at this crackling object, they found themselves filled with fear—and it felt like a fear greater than even the unusual circumstances should merit. It was almost as if the object was somehow tapping into their emotions and purposefully triggering their fear response.

Fighting through her terror, Gwen grabbed her flashlight and turned it on. With shaking hands, she tried to shine it up at their frightening visitor, but the shining blue ball reacted instantly and took evasive action before the flashlight beam could illuminate it. The orb shot off into the trees for cover before flying upward and disappearing over the horizon. Whatever the object was, it obviously had no use for Gwen's flashlight beam—this craft was there to watch, not to be watched.

Understandably, Terry and Gwen were thoroughly shaken by the experience. They called it a night and hurried back to what they thought would be the safety of their home. But no more than two hours passed before they noticed a strange blue glow outside of their window. Then, to their horror, the same blue ball sailed past toward the back of their house. As it did so, the lights of the house began to dim and brighten slightly, as if the softball-sized object was somehow affecting the electrical supply.

Terry and Gwen rushed to the door to look outside. They saw the strange floating probe flying several hundred feet away before disappearing from sight. But this wasn't the last the Shermans would see of these strange, probing balls of light—and their next encounter with these otherworldly reconnaissance craft would be a lethal one.

Last Stand at the Ranch House

As frightening as the happenings on the ranch had been at times, to that point they had not caused any physical harm. The strange blue orbs in particular seemed content just to watch the

Shermans and their animals from a distance; they had never given them any reason to think that their very lives might be in danger. But in April of 1996, what was meant to be a quiet evening of relaxation turned into a night of sheer terror.

Terry had been sitting outside enjoying the evening breeze with his three loyal guard dogs when his peace was interrupted by the now eerily familiar flash of blue which signified the arrival of one of the orbs which had been visiting on a regular basis. His dogs, perhaps aware of the intruding object even before he was, were already growling and whining at the sight. The object was hovering just a few feet off the ground, and it appeared to be approaching them. When it was less than 100 yards away from Terry and his dogs, it abruptly changed course and started heading north.

Terry had reached a breaking point. He was now entirely fed up with these intrusions, and against his better judgment, he sicced his dogs on the orb. The dogs took off at full speed and easily caught up to the slow-moving object. While the object could easily have shot up into the air to avoid the dogs, it seemed to be somehow playing along with the pursuit, dropping down just within striking distance of the hounds' eager jaws.

The shining sphere seemed to be showing off its maneuverability by allowing the dogs to come close to biting down on it, only to artfully dodge their fangs with split-second precision. This infuriated the dogs, which at this point probably wouldn't have returned even if Terry had called them. Their singular focus was to sink their teeth into this alien (for lack of a better word) piece of technology that was tormenting them. All the while, the orb was purposefully leading the pursuing pack into the thick tree cover to the south, as if it wanted the game to continue away from Terry's worried eyes.

Sure enough, the orb suddenly dropped to the ground, tantalizingly within reach of the chasing dogs, and sped off into the woods. All three dogs followed in hot pursuit. Terry's beloved pets had left his sight for the last time, as mere moments later he heard what could only be their death wails: three howls of brief but intense pain. Terry stared hard and horrified at the entrance to the woods, but he could not hear or see anything more. The entire ranch was now gripped in a deathly quiet.

Terry sat in his lawn chair for the better part of two hours as the darkness grew around him, hoping beyond hope to see his dogs come running back. And as brave as Terry had proved himself to be in his encounter with the "bullet-proof wolf", he didn't dare step into those dark woods where the hovering menace still lurked. Eventually he quietly packed up his things and went in for the night.

It was not until the next morning, under the comforting shield of the daylight sun, that Terry finally ventured into the forest. As soon as he stepped within the ring of trees he was greeted with the distinct odor of death. Whatever he might find, it wouldn't be good. After only a few more steps through the maze of trees he found the source of the putrid scent and recoiled in horror at the sight of three oval piles of incinerated flesh on the forest floor. It was clear that the shining blue probe had expertly herded the dogs out of sight inside the woods and then turned on them and viciously incinerated them.

With the loss of his beloved dogs to the increasingly malevolent phenomena besieging Skinwalker Ranch, Terry finally caved to the pressure. As he walked away from the nightmarish sight the strange intelligence had left behind, he knew it wouldn't be long before his family would be forced to walk away from the ranch completely. The hidden forces that had long resided within Skinwalker Ranch were now evicting the latest residents.

How Robert Bigelow Bought the Farm

After the death of their dogs, the Shermans were at their wits' end. With nothing to lose, they finally broke their silence about what was happening on their ranch. Their story first appeared in a 1996 edition of a local newspaper, the *Deseret News*, and this rendition of the tale caught the attention of billionaire Las Vegas businessman Robert Bigelow.

Bigelow had made his fortune as owner of the Budget Suites hotel chain, but he had many other interests besides the hospitality industry—and one of those interests was the paranormal. Just one year before the Skinwalker Ranch story hit the paper, Bigelow had founded a paranormal research organization called the National Institute for Discovery Science (NIDS). This group was tasked with investigating a host of mysterious and strange phenomena to find concrete evidence in all kinds of nebulous subject matter that had hitherto remained elusive.

So when Robert Bigelow received word of the strange happenings on the Sherman Ranch, he was immediately intrigued. He had already been considering the creation of a NIDS research outpost somewhere in the western United States, and so the chance to purchase land that had been the focal point of such unexplainable activity was the proverbial icing on his paranormal cake. He came to terms with the Shermans within a matter of weeks, and the sale of Skinwalker Ranch was finalized in September of 1996.

But that didn't happen before the mysterious forces left a final parting gift to the Shermans—and this time, the manifestation was more personal than ever. Terry Sherman later claimed that after one of their last nights sleeping at the Ranch, both he and his wife woke up with the telltale sign of alien abduction—a scoop mark scar mysteriously appearing on one's body.

The day before this incident they had spent the whole day taking care of their cattle and preparing their ranch for the impending handover to Bigelow. When the weary couple went inside for the night, they made sure they shut their house up tight, locking all the doors and even the windows. After a long, hot shower to wash away the grime of the day, they went to bed early. They woke up the next morning to see their bed sheets soaked in blood. As they were wriggling out of these inexplicably bloody sheets, they noticed that they both had matching scoop marks on their right thumbs.

Needless to say, the Shermans were relieved to finally be leaving the ranch. They took the money from the sale and used it to purchase another ranch some 20 miles away. But as grateful as they were for their escape from Skinwalker Ranch, there was a part of Terry that just couldn't let the ranch go completely. You can chock it up to his rancher's pride, but Terry couldn't quite stomach the idea of letting the mysterious phenomena win. Even after moving out, he still wanted to get to the bottom of what was happening.

And so Terry signed on with NIDS to become an extra ranch hand and assist in the investigations being carried out by the team of researchers. The arrangement was just as appealing to Bigelow, who knew that no one knew the grounds better than Terry and considered him an invaluable resource. One of Terry's first major tasks as Skinwalker Ranch guide for NIDS was looking into a recent spate of cattle mutilations.

Such things were not exactly unusual in the region; cattle mutilations had been reported in and around Skinwalker Ranch ever since the 1960s. The Shermans' first possible encounter with the phenomenon had occurred in April of 1995. The ranch had just endured several days of heavy rain, and Terry and his son were attempting to gather their cattle on the slippery range.

While they were trying to retrieve a wayward calf, they spotted a cow struggling to pull herself up a steep incline, but miserably failing due to the slick mud that covered the field. Terry decided to take care of the cow after they caught the calf. But when the Shermans returned to the cow just minutes later, they found it lying down at the bottom of the ridge, completely lifeless.

They initially surmised that it had drowned in the flood waters, but upon closer inspection they could see that the animal had been mutilated in every sense of the word. Its anus, genitals, and tongue had all been sliced out as if with a surgeon's scalpel. The poor beast had also been completely drained of blood.

Several more mysteriously mutilated cattle were found after the NIDS takeover, and the mutilations invariably occurred when no one was looking. In one instance, two mutilated animals were discovered at approximately the same time within several feet of each other, with their carcasses shoved up under a fence. Terry scoured the vicinity and helped to secure the perimeter, but nothing was found. Security cameras were then installed throughout the area, and an observation trailer was set up from which trained scientists could observe anything that transpired on the ranch.

But inexplicably, they had seen nothing when on January 21, 1997, Terry discovered young cows near the observation center with strange wounds to their eyes and ears. The injuries seemed to have occurred during a bad snow storm the night before. Had the entities behind the injuries taken advantage of the near white-out conditions to cut into these animals? And if so, why hadn't they finished the job? Had someone on the research staff gotten too close and sent them fleeing?

At any rate, the heavy snowfall meant that there were no footprints to be found. Unable to find a trail leading to the culprits, Terry summoned local veterinarians to take a look at the affected cattle. The first vet took one look at the injuries and declared that they were unlike anything he'd ever encountered before. But the next veterinarian, a more experienced man, strenuously disagreed. He insisted that the wounds had been made by a coyote or a wildcat. The idea of a big cat randomly attacking cattle during a snowstorm struck the NIDS team as unlikely, but such theories from veterinarians and other local professionals were quite common. Often enough, when they were confronted with the phenomenon of cattle mutilations, they would simply try to explain it way—even if the explanation didn't make a whole lot of sense.

Whatever their origin, the mutilations only increased after this point. In one particularly harrowing incident, one of Terry's own calves (which he had recently transferred back to Skinwalker Ranch) was viciously mutilated in broad daylight while Terry and other researchers were standing within arm's reach. Terry was anguished at the sight, but the research team didn't have time for sympathy. They got busy studying the carcass, then conducted an autopsy to find out how the animal had met its end.

The calf's body appeared to have been torn open by some tremendous energy. One leg had been ripped off right at the joint as easily as someone would pull the leg off of a cooked rotisserie chicken. No known predator of the animal world would have been able to do such a thing with the leg of a living, struggling cow. Besides this dismemberment, the calf had the typical hallmarks of cattle mutilation. All its internal organs had been removed with laser precision, it was completely drained of blood, and one ear was neatly severed from the head. There was no obvious ripping or tearing at the incision, and when the wound was placed under a microscope it was irrefutably clear that the ear had been cut off with a precision instrument. Bigelow's NIDS had a real and active predator—of the paranormal kind.

Higher Dimensions

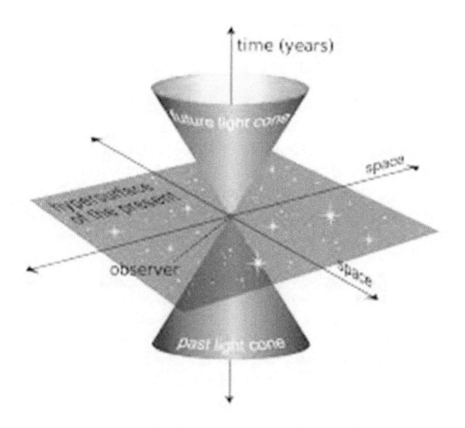

After living on Skinwalker Ranch for a while, the Sherman family had begun to notice discernible patterns in the paranormal activity that confronted them. And the biggest canvas for these telltale signs was always the skies above their heads. In particular, a piece of sky right over a wooded grove hosted a very specific retinue of spooky happenings. Almost every evening, like clockwork, right when the sun was going down, an odd-looking orange smudge would appear just above the treetops.

At first the family rationalized this aerial phenomenon as merely an odd manifestation of the refraction of setting sunlight as it passed over the clouds. But as this phenomenon repeated itself without alteration night after night, Terry's curiosity was piqued enough to investigate further. Setting his night-vision-equipped rifle on a tree stump, he used the weapon's scope to zoom in on the orange smudge suspended over the trees.

Strangely, as he looked more closely at the group of orange clouds, he could almost look *through* them to what appeared to be "another sky". He seemed to be looking down a tunnel that opened up outside the very fabric of space and time! Was he viewing a doorway to another dimension? Was this tunnel, spanning from one world to another, where the strange vehicles, creatures and other entities were arriving from?

Just a few days later, Terry witnessed what appeared to be a verification of this theory. As he stared through his rifle's scope once more, he saw a large, black, triangle-shaped craft fly out of the putative interdimensional doorway. This doorway was apparently paper-thin around the edges and could only be seen when looked at straight on. This meant that anyone driving along the roadways near the property would not be able to see it, but it could be clearly observed from within the ranch.

Is the Skinwalker Ranch home to naturally (or even unnaturally) occurring doorways into another dimension? Are advanced aircraft, otherwise known as UFOs routinely entering our world through these interdimensional portals? If so, the craft weren't the only things shimmying through these galactic gateways. Later witnesses have even seen humanoid creatures stepping out of these open doorways into our dimension.

In August of 1997, the NIDS crew witnessed something highly unusual even by the standards of Skinwalker Ranch. It was three in the morning, and two scientists named Mike and Jim had been manning an observation post for several hours when they saw an unknown light shining in the distant darkness. Well aware that something unusual was occurring in front of them, the men set up a camera on a tripod to capture the incident. As the camera automatically snapped pictures every 30 seconds, Mike peered out at the anomaly through a pair of night vision binoculars.

As the scientist stared in disbelief, the light turned into a circular portal or tunnel. Moments later, Mike shouted in shock, "Jesus Christ! Something's in the tunnel!" This was soon followed by the exclamation, "Oh my God, it just climbed out!" Mike was watching a large humanoid creature tumble out of the strange interdimensional doorway that periodically appeared over Skinwalker Ranch.

With no binoculars of his own, Jim could not see this detail. All he could see was a swirling vortex of light, and that light was now rapidly shrinking, collapsing in on itself, before disappearing entirely.

Based on Mike's observation through the binoculars, it would seem that the portal was open just long enough for the entity to walk through it. Immediately after the being crossed over, the interdimensional door shut behind it. But despite Mike's startling testimony, none of the NIDS equipment was able to pick up hard evidence of this bizarre event.

The photos showed nothing more than a distant, indistinct light, and other sensitive equipment deployed in the area to pick up fluctuations in X-rays, gamma rays, beta rays and the like failed to pick up anything of significance either. The next day NIDS crew members scoured the ground over which the light had been seen for footprints from the entity that had dropped out of the tunnel, but none were ever found.

For the time being, this event rests solely on the testimony of one rattled NIDS researcher. But as strange as it sounds, Skinwalker Ranch may not be the only location where these interdimensional doorways occur. Just take for example a case that came to light in January of 2014, in which a Wisconsin rancher named Leroy Smith reportedly witnessed a very similar phenomenon. The winter was particularly bad in Wisconsin that year, with a frigid blast of arctic air perpetually blanketing much of the rancher's property in ice and snow.

Leroy says that the strange happenings usually occurred when the snowstorms were at their worst. Much like Terry Sherman's experience on Skinwalker Ranch, the phenomenon would begin with an orange vortex-like structure appearing over the horizon, just above the treetops. This structure was only visible from one direction; that is, it could only be seen when looking at it head-on. From the sides, this bizarre tunnel of light was so thin it was almost two-dimensional.

Head-on, however, the old rancher could stare in amazement as the tunnel opened up in the middle of the sky and creatures dropped out of it. Yes, that's right. This Wisconsin rancher saw big, hairy creatures descend from the spinning sky vortex. He also saw creatures much more akin to the traditional skin-walker: dog-like animals that would jump from the opening, hit the ground and then take off running on two legs. Although Wisconsin is admittedly a bit removed from the traditional source of skin-walker lore in the southwestern United States, the bipedal dogs Leroy describes have an undeniable similarity to the shape-shifting dog-men of Navajo legend.

One interesting difference between the sightings that occurred on Leroy Smith's ranch in Wisconsin and those at the Skinwalker Ranch in Utah is that whatever dropped out of the Wisconsin portals left footprints behind. The fresh footprints in the snow looked exactly as if they had been made by an ordinary flesh-and-blood being, but strangely enough, they would begin out of nowhere. It was as if whatever made them had just dropped out of the sky—exactly as Leroy describes. Attempts to track this creature were fruitless, however, as the trail of the beast would disappear just as suddenly as it had begun.

Before NIDS was shut down in 2007, the team had one more encounter with a portal on Skinwalker Ranch—but rather than seeing something drop out of it, this time they witnessed a strange Bigfoot-like creature jump into a portal! On this occasion, the researchers and ranch hands were in hot pursuit of a strange, hairy, bipedal creature. Incredibly, just when the Bigfoot seemed to have been cornered, it ran up a hill, jumped into a large orange tunnel that appeared out of thin air, and disappeared.

The entire tunnel immediately vanished as well. It seemed as if the being had created an opening in the fabric of space and time at will, and then, as soon as it had crossed over, shut the door behind it so no one could follow. If true, this mind-bending phenomenon is proof positive that whoever serves as interdimensional doorman at Skinwalker Ranch is in complete control.

Skin-Walkers and Vandals

As well funded as Bigelow's study of the Skinwalker Ranch was, as the 1990s drew to a close, the team of investigators seemed no closer to getting to the bottom of things than when they had first arrived.

From the very beginning, former owner and current ranch hand Terry Sherman had insisted that the research should be approached like a hunter stalking wild game. He believed that since whatever was behind the phenomena was obviously watching their actions, any overt show of cameras and other instruments would make the unknown force go into hiding. Terry advocated employing as much stealth as possible, only using minimal equipment, and setting up discreet viewing posts far away from each other.

The NIDS researchers did not follow this advice, however. Instead, they installed cameras all throughout the property, set to film just about every square inch of terrain 24 hours a day. But just as Terry had feared, as soon as these cameras were put in place, the camera-shy skin-walkers made themselves scarce.

In one area that had previously been a hotbed of activity, a total of six sophisticated surveillance cameras were installed. Previously this location had been beset by almost all of the standard skin-walker activity, including cattle mutilations, flying blue balls of light, strange aircraft, and the infamous portals that opened up over the horizon. The six cameras were set to film every section of this paranormal paradise 24/7. But just as Terry had feared, all of this equipment seemed to make the unknown force go dormant. After several months of filming, nothing of any significance had been captured on tape.

Before the cameras were installed, many members of the research staff had personally witnessed bizarre phenomena taking place. But as soon as the cameras went up, the game was over, and the power behind the skin-walkers decided to lie low. For about a year, everything was so low-key that some began to think that the presence that had been haunting the ranch had simply moved on and left the area for good. The silence was finally broken on July 20, 1998, when Terry Sherman, who was on duty at the command and control center, was made aware of an unsettling occurrence.

Half of the cameras tasked with filming the terrain had been knocked out simultaneously. It had been storming heavily the past few days, so Terry naturally assumed that there was some kind of electrical failure due to the rain or thunderstorms. He went to inspect the downed cameras to see the damage—and found that while the cameras were indeed damaged, it was not by lighting.

To his amazement, he saw that the three cameras which had gone offline had all of their wiring forcefully ripped out. It looked like a bad case of vandalism or sabotage—but the fact that the equipment had been so expertly torn asunder from 15 feet in the air made that seem highly improbable. All of the cameras were positioned atop 15-foot wooden poles, so any conventional saboteur would have had to scale the poles to rip out the wires.

Climbing up a narrow pole and holding on to the smooth wood while tearing out the thick wiring would be a practically superhuman feat. The wires had been held in place by thick PVC pipes that ran down to the foot of the poles, but all of these had been expertly detached. Each of the three disabled cameras had been afflicted with identical damage.

The other three cameras, however, remained completely operational, and so the NIDS group turned to them to find out just what had happened. Fortunately, one of them had been pointed directly at one of the sabotaged cameras. The investigators immediately replayed the video from the time that they believed the vandalism had occurred. But incredibly, as they watched the footage, they could see absolutely nothing out of the ordinary.

Perplexed, the researchers sent the tape to a lab in Las Vegas to have it digitally enhanced. The enhancement revealed the red recording lights on the damaged cameras, and this proved to be important, because the footage indicated that all three affected cameras had switched off simultaneously at 8:30 PM. But still, there was no perpetrator to be seen. The only conclusion the NIDS researchers could draw was that whoever had damaged the cameras was endowed with the power to render themselves invisible!

One person who had no trouble believing this incredible theory was Terry Sherman—for this was not the first time he had witnessed the camouflage ability of the skin-walkers inhabiting his ranch. Both he and his son had seen it firsthand in 1996, shortly after the Shermans' story was published in the *Deseret News* and just as paranormal enthusiasts were beginning to take note. One such enthusiast arrived unannounced at their door in June of that year, asking to spend time and "meditate" on the ranch. Terry was slightly amused by the request, so he went ahead and gave permission, thinking that nothing would come of it.

Picking a pristine pasture near the woods, the man began to meditate just as he'd said. He stood in the middle of the clearing, raised his hands toward the heavens, and with his eyes closed tight, began to focus on his inward being. While he was deep in this trance-like state, a sudden violent rustling of trees came from the woods. The man, lost in his meditation, did not seem to notice, but the Shermans watched the disturbance with increasing alarm.

To their astonishment, they saw an almost completely invisible figure emerge from the trees. Due to a strange, pixelated effect, as if sunlight was being directed around it, the entity was so blurry that they could just barely make out its outline as it crossed the field in broad daylight. As they watched in stunned silence, the camouflaged being picked up speed and ran straight toward the meditating visitor. Before anyone could quite process what was happening, the entity stopped right in front of the visitor and erupted into a roar of aggression. The meditating man fell to the ground in shock at what he was seeing and hearing. After the deafening roar, the semi-invisible entity simply turned around and ran back into the woods from whence it had come.

Coincidentally enough, Terry and his son watched the Arnold Schwarzenegger / Jesse Ventura film *Predator* just a few months later and were struck by similarity between this real-life entity's capability and that of the fictional character in the film. In the movie, the alien predator uses an advanced cloaking device to make itself invisible. Were the entities on Skinwalker Ranch utilizing a similar technology? Is that how they managed to dismantle three complex surveillance stations without being seen, and without being recorded on the remaining cameras?

It just might be, because scientists now believe that such means of camouflage is not as farfetched as previously thought. Researchers all over the planet are currently perfecting methods of bending sunlight over objects in order to render them invisible. If we are beginning to master this technology ourselves, then it should not surprise us that another, far more advanced intelligence would have developed such capabilities as well. Perhaps it was such advanced technology that made it so easy for the paranormal denizens of Skinwalker Ranch to stay one step ahead of Bigelow and his associates.

Further Developments

Towards the end of the NIDS era at Skinwalker Ranch, the most frequent intruders were not of the paranormal kind, but of the bored teenager kind. The ranch's notoriety had begun to attract trespassers and thrill seekers with some regularity. In 2006, one of these trespassers was UFO enthusiast Ryan Skinner, who had first learned of the ranch by accident.

Skinner had been on a road trip with his girlfriend when he happened upon flying orbs very similar to those seen on Skinwalker Ranch. After he returned from this harrowing first encounter, he found out that his car had been passing through the vicinity of the ranch at the time. Intrigued by what he had seen, Skinner was determined to go back. He had always been searching for a place to hunt the paranormal, and Skinwalker Ranch seemed to have his name all over it. He began to make frequent nighttime trips out to the property, and on many of these nocturnal forays he met with the strange glowing balls of light.

During one of these encounters, Skinner was hidden on a ridge watching as the objects seemed to be observing the cattle grazing below. The surrounding lighting suddenly began to flicker before going out completely. Shortly thereafter, the door to one of the trailers next to the grazing cattle was flung open and a security guard came crashing through it with a litany of profanity. The guard made a beeline for a transformer box and fiddled around for a minute or so before the lights snapped back on.

The most interesting thing about this is that Skinner saw one of the balls of light turn its attention away from the cows and fly over to the guard. According to Skinner, the ball of light hovered right behind the guard as he worked without him ever realizing it. After the guard went inside, the orb hung in the air over the trailer as if it was thinking about what its next move should be. Then it darted off to join the larger group of orbs that had been slinking around the ranch.

Skinner's account seems to verify that as much as NIDS attempted to document and verify all of the strange happenings on the Skinwalker Ranch, the phenomena were always one step ahead of them. It was this very fact that led the scientists at NIDS to come up with perhaps the most startling conclusion of all—that they were dealing with a "pre-cognitive" intelligence. Many have erroneously asserted that paranormal activity at the ranch disappeared when the scientists arrived. But it didn't. It merely changed its tactics.

NIDS saw very much the same phenomena that the Sherman family did, but the activity was so randomized and erratic that they could never capture any hard evidence. If cameras and other data collecting equipment were placed on one side of the property, the manifestations would just shift to the other. Those involved became increasingly aware of an extremely selective intelligence at work, hampering their investigation. This intelligence would pick and choose who it revealed itself to and what times and places the manifestations would occur.

But most startling of all, it seemed to be able to predict the actions of the NIDS crew before they were implemented. If you moved left, the phenomena would move right. It knew what you were going to do before you even dreamed up the action in the first place. Before you even thought to move your right foot forward, this strange pre-cognitive intelligence was already registering and tracking your movement. The NIDS scientists assert that it is for this reason that they were never able to get any hard data on the phenomena of Skinwalker Ranch.

Now, you may be tempted to think that that's merely a handy excuse for their distinct lack of results. But before you start scoffing, you may want to consider some of the stranger things that quantum physicists have learned about the very fabric of our reality—and how we perceive that reality. Because one of the major discoveries of quantum physics is that at the quantum level, things actually do change and react to our own observations.

As hard as it may be to grasp such a strange concept, the veracity of this theory has been proven time and time again in laboratories all around the world. It has been found that at the quantum level, light waves can spontaneously become particles and vice versa, as well as move from one location to another, simply because they are observed. If these fundamental building blocks of reality change upon observation, how much more could other aspects of our reality bend and adjust as we observe them?

It was actually Colonel John Alexander who coined the phrase "pre-cognitive sentient intelligence" with regard to Skinwalker Ranch. During the Vietnam War, Col. Alexander—the inspiration for the George Clooney / Ewan McGregor / Jeff Bridges / Kevin Spacey film *The Men Who Stare at Goats*—was part of a special forces unit attempting to create supersoldiers through metaphysical exercises such as transcendental meditation and the like. After his time in Vietnam, Col. Alexander became an intelligence officer and worked on classified studies of UFOs for the U.S. military. If anyone might know a little something about cracking the thin veil of what we normally perceive to be reality, Col. Alexander would be the one, and his rather grim assessment of what was happening at the Skinwalker Ranch was that they were dealing with a "trickster" entity which was merely toying with them as it saw fit.

It is interesting to note that this "trickster" motif—the idea that otherworldly entities come into our reality just to play pranks on us—can be found in ancient folklore all around the world. Look into the tales of leprechauns and Loki, elves and Anansi, and yes, the Navajo legend of the skin-walker, and you will be inundated with accounts of a precognitive intelligence doing its best to get one over on mankind. If Col. Alexander is right, perhaps the whole ordeal of Skinwalker Ranch was simply one big, long-drawn-out—Gotcha!

Possible Explanations

As we bring this book to a close, let's examine some explanations that have been posited for what is really going on at Skinwalker Ranch. These explanations range from the prosaic, to the enigmatic and deceptive, to the fantastic, and to the even more fantastic. Here is a brief run-through of theories that have been proposed by experts and enthusiasts alike.

Massive Military PSYOPs Program

Terry Sherman himself has long suspected that his former property was a secret military testing ground. He feels that users of advanced military technology, ranging from stealth aircraft to man-portable cloaking devices, were running amok on the ranch. And their behavior seemed to indicate that the residents and their psychological reactions to the phenomena were very much a part of the experiment.

But could this be true? Could the military really be testing exotic cutting-edge technologies over the idyllic backdrop of a rural ranch? If this is the case, the testing has been going on for quite some time, perhaps since the 1930s. This does not quite account for the earlier legends of bipedal dog-men, but it does correspond with the UFO activity of more recent times.

Interestingly, the 1930s was the decade when the Myers family first bought the farm. Now, the curious thing about the Myers is the fact that they never reported anything unusual during their many decades at the ranch. The Shermans, meanwhile, experienced odd behavior from the moment they moved in. For the more conspiracy minded among us, this can lead to only one conclusion—the Myers were in on it!

For those who believe that the ranch has been part of a massive military PSYOPs program spanning several decades, it would seem plausible that the Myers family long ago signed on the dotted line to take part. But whether the Myers were in on the plot or not, the real question is—why? What was the goal of all of these operations? Was it to test human reaction to advanced holographic displays and cutting-edge camouflage technology?

If so, it would hardly be the first time that a remote region in the West was used for military testing. Just think of all the atomic bombs and covert military hardware tested in remote deserts in Nevada and New Mexico. Utah could work just as well as the desolate backdrop for such secretive military operations; much of it is far off the grid, with few potential witnesses around. It's the perfect place to test something out on just a few select individuals at a time—and the Skinwalker Ranch phenomena were certainly selective about when and where they decided to manifest.

But even assuming that the Myers had agreed to be subjected to such testing when they built their first ranch house in the 1930s, the Shermans most certainly did not know or agree to any such arrangement. To continue such testing on the new residents without their consent would have been a severe violation of legal protocol. The only hint the Shermans were given before moving in that there might be some kind of military involvement with the property was when Garth Myers, who had inherited the ranch from the original owners, mysteriously advised Terry to avoid digging on the property.

This directive would make sense if it was possible that excavations could uncover underground installations. The idea of military bases being buried underground in the vast expanse of the western United States is no conspiracy-theory fantasy; during the Cold War, several bunker-type command centers were buried all over the West to prepare for nuclear war. Terry must have known of this possibility, but to think that such an underground base might be buried underneath the ranch was still unsettling.

And it certainly didn't help matters that one of the very first of the wide range of odd phenomena was strange underground pounding sounds. These would be followed by the sounds of drilling and heavy machinery working feverishly right underneath the Shermans' feet at all hours of the day. Just who was performing these subterranean maneuvers? Did the Shermans and those who followed after them become the unwitting pawns in a series of clandestine military maneuvers?

If you can accept the stranger Skinwalker Ranch phenomena—the portals, the balls of light, the wolves of unusual size—as being the product of advanced holographs or maybe even mental manipulation, then massive military PSYOPs could indeed serve as a somewhat rational explanation. But then again, nothing is ever quite rational in regard to Skinwalker Ranch!

Native American Curse

The oldest explanation for strange happenings in the region of Utah where Skinwalker Ranch is located comes from the oldest residents of the region: the Native American tribes. In particular, the Ute and the Navajo have a long backstory as to just how the land of the Uinta Basin became cursed. You see, these two peoples were competitors and archrivals before Europeans ever set foot in the Americas. It is out of this friction and conflict that the lore of the skin-walker originates in the oral histories of both tribes.

These histories contend that the Navajos were finally defeated by the Utes and forced to leave their land in the Uinta Basin. According to the story, the Navajo knew they had to go, but they weren't going to leave without a parting gift to their enemies—a gift in the form of a curse. Supposedly, before the Navajo surrendered their land to the Utes, they placed a curse on it that brought forth the dreaded skin-walker and all of the frightful activity that came with it.

The traditional belief systems of many Native American tribes place much emphasis on blessings and curses carried out by mystical shamans. Terry Sherman himself once came upon the recent remains of what appeared to be a Native American tribal ritual on the grounds of Skinwalker Ranch. He wasn't sure who had snuck onto his property to perform it, but it certainly had all the hallmarks of a traditional religious ceremony. Were local tribespeople sneaking onto the ranch to fend off the curse—or were they adding to it?

Belief in the power of curses is still strong among the locals, and so is the belief in skin-walkers, but despite all of the attempts to link the activity at the ranch to Native American, lore there is one aspect of the story that just doesn't fit. The skin-walker of Navajo legend is a brutal, ruthless fiend who wouldn't hesitate to strike a person dead. But as far as we know, the phenomena on Skinwalker Ranch have never killed a single human being.

The activity has claimed the lives of plenty of animals, including Terry's beloved pets, but even though the presence at the ranch has melted dogs and mutilated cattle, it has stayed its hand when it comes to physically harming humanity. People have felt ill effects such as headaches and nosebleeds, and as was the case with the Sherman family, sometimes strange marks would appear on their bodies. However, no mortal harm has come to any man, woman, or child. This restraint goes against the traditional portrayal of the bloodthirsty skin-walker. Nevertheless, the legend of the curse still persists, and as has often been said—a curse is as strong as those who believe it.

Unknown Form of Consciousness

After nearly a decade of studying the elusive activity on the ranch, the NIDS group more or less came to the consensus that they were dealing with an unknown form of consciousness—some sort of massive collective consciousness whose senses could monitor the entire ranch 24 hours a day. Indeed, as much as they tried to observe the paranormal manifestations, this collective consciousness seemed to be much better equipped to observe the researchers themselves! Whatever inhabited the ranch was always at least two steps ahead of the NIDS crew, anticipating their actions before they made them.

The Shermans had often felt that the presence was actively eavesdropping on them, and this belief was apparently confirmed when the intelligence reacted to an offhand remark Gwen had made. She had briefly mentioned to Terry her fear of something bad happening to her prized new bulls. Immediately afterward, Terry went outside and was shocked to find that those very bulls were nowhere to be seen. Their frantic search for the animals would conclude with one of the most infamous incidents that occurred during their time at the ranch.

They ultimately found their missing bulls, but the condition in which they found them defied explanation. The animals were discovered impossibly lined up and neatly placed into a locked trailer. Not only that, they were staring off into space as if they were somehow "switched off" and in a complete trance, oblivious to the world around them. The very second the astonished Terry Sherman opened the trailer, the bulls came to life as if someone had just hit the Play button to bring these freeze-frame creatures back to reality.

The idea of a sentient precognitive intelligence eventually became the prevailing theory among the NIDS researchers. Their findings pointed to the conclusion that an unknown intelligence which could predict events was attempting to interact with people in a variety of ways. In particular, this unknown form of consciousness often tried to produce very specific emotive responses from those it manipulated.

Sometimes it did this in subtle ways, through trickery, and at other times it employed more direct means. The more direct approach was experienced early on by Terry and Gwen after one of the shining blue probe-like orbs confronted them. Terry believes that the probe somehow tapped into his mind and deliberately instilled fear into him and his wife. They were instantly filled with terror and dread, as if someone had flipped a switch. Trespasser Ryan Skinner had a similar experience later on when one of these probes hovered over him and sent instantaneous shockwaves of fear coursing through his body. This was not fear that came from him, but fear that seemed to have been unnaturally injected into him from the outside.

An unknown intelligence playing games and manipulating our emotions? According to the official findings of NIDS, as strange as it all may sound, that's the most likely explanation.

Interference from Parallel Universe

Whether the general public wants to accept it or not, most modern physicists firmly believe that we are part of a multiverse with several slightly similar yet different parallel universes bumping up against our own. The nuts and bolts of quantum mechanics is a bit too much to get into here, but just know that these experts agree that our very reality is most likely separated from a multitude of other potential realities by merely a thin membrane of dark matter.

If this theory is correct, is it possible that some advanced species from the "universe next door" has found a way to punch through that thin barrier of separation? Is Skinwalker Ranch a place where the thin membrane that separates universes has been successfully traversed?

According to eyewitness testimony from both the Shermans and the NIDS researchers, random portals have appeared above the landscape on several occasions, and UFOs and strange creatures crossed through them. And they were not the first to witness such things in the region. Local Native American lore has long described the appearance of doorways to other worlds. It is an integral and accepted part of their belief system; perhaps we could learn to accept it too.

Extraterrestrial Incursion

Among UFO buffs, the most popular explanation for the happenings at Skinwalker Ranch is, of course, an extraterrestrial incursion. Although many aspects of the Skinwalker phenomena differ from the typical ET narrative, diehard believers have come up with a variety of explanations for these discrepancies. Some suggest that the aliens are conducting psychological experiments on those who wander onto the ranch—just like the military PSYOPs explanation, except it's an alien military behind it!

Other ET believers take a simpler approach, postulating that ETs are behind a large part of the activity at the ranch, but not all of it. They argue that there is indeed something unusual about Skinwalker Ranch—so unusual that extraterrestrials are drawn to it for their own research purposes, thereby compounding the oddity of the location even further.

The Shermans witnessed a wide variety of strange craft hovering over the ranch, and Terry observed some that seemed to scan the grounds of the property as if they were looking for something. Gwen even saw one of the occupants of such a craft, a strange looking man decked out in some sort of uniform or flight suit, sitting at a desk! Perhaps these ETs are scientists who are just exploring a strange feature of our planet.

The probes that seem to monitor the ranch could also be hypothesized as being extraterrestrial in origin. Are these the robotic scouts of alien explorers? Artificially intelligent drones sent by ET to gather data on the Earth and its inhabitants? Most scientists do believe that the first contact with an extraterrestrial civilization would probably be with one of its far-flung autonomous explorers. But other than a few blurry photos, so far there is no concrete evidence to support this theory.

Mental Mirages and Hallucinations

It has been postulated for some time that perhaps there is something at the Skinwalker Ranch—in the environment itself, perhaps—that affects the minds of residents and visitors alike. Perhaps intense magnetic fields or some other naturally occurring phenomenon could be creating mental mirages and hallucinations. This could explain a wide array of events, and also explain why these events cannot be captured on camera—because they exist only in someone's fevered mind.

But this explanation falls short on many fronts. The fact that multiple people have witnessed the same events at the same time pretty much rules out individual hallucinations. Also, the phenomena have had very real physical ramifications—consider the Shermans' incinerated dogs, the mutilated cattle, and the destruction of the cameras. This seems to prove that, as crazy as the activity on the ranch may be, it's most likely not all in our heads!

Widespread Deception

For those who have not experienced the bizarre occurrences at Skinwalker Ranch firsthand, perhaps the most convenient explanation of all is to say that the whole thing was simply made up! Those who adhere to this theory believe that the Shermans created the modern mythology of the ranch by piggybacking on local UFO sightings and older Native American legends. They claim that the Shermans came up with a creative storyline to attract attention to their property so that someone would buy it.

According to this theory, they didn't sell to escape the paranormal, but to escape a failed business venture. You see, the Shermans' profits had nosedived immediately before they sold the ranch, and as unusual as such a marketing strategy would be, the strange tales they told did indeed attract a buyer—Mr. Robert Bigelow, who paid the Shermans a handsome amount of money for their property. This big payout would have been the motivating factor for the initial deception.

But in order for widespread deception to be a plausible explanation, it would have to be very widespread indeed. The Shermans are not the only people claiming to have witnessed strange events on the ranch. Many visitors, and a whole team of research scientists, would have to be in on the deception in order for it to work. And most would contend that such a vast conspiracy is just as farfetched as the bizarre stories told about the ranch in the first place.

More Questions than Answers

Hotel chain owner and Bigelow Aerospace founder Robert Bigelow pulled the plug on his NIDS operations at Skinwalker Ranch in 2004. Not a whole lot is known about his decision-making process, but it is said that funding for the project began to dry up. Bigelow had been given several governmental grants for the research, but when these were not renewed, he seemed to lose interest.

Interestingly enough, however, it was immediately after Bigelow shut down operations on the ranch that Bigelow Aerospace began to really take off. Bigelow began to partner directly with NASA for the creation of special modules and additions for the International Space Station, and contracts are currently in the works to install his Bigelow Expandable Activity Module (BEAM) in the space station by 2020.

However, it's some of the lesser known government projects that Bigelow became involved with after shutting down Skinwalker Ranch that have gotten the most attention lately. Foremost among these is a Pentagon UFO study that just came to light in December of 2017. Known as the Advanced Aviation Threat Initiative (AAVTI), this program began in 2007 when Bigelow convinced his longtime political crony, Senate Majority Leader Harry Reid, to seek funding for an official inquiry into UFOs. Such a thing hadn't been done since the shutdown of the Air Force's UFO study, Project Blue Book, in 1969, but Reid managed to get funding for the project diverted to Bigelow Aerospace anyway—to the tune of approximately 22 million dollars between 2007 and 2012.

During these years the study researched credible UFO sightings by military personnel and other trained professionals—some of which were captured on camera—along with unknown metal fragments and alloys allegedly left behind by UFOs. Bigelow stashed the evidence in converted buildings, and all of this—22 million in taxpayer dollars notwithstanding—was done in complete secret from the public.

This secrecy led the program's research head, Luis Elizondo, to resign from his post in October of 2017, just before the bombshell broke. Elizondo sent his letter of resignation to the Trump Administration's Secretary of Defense Jim Mattis, explaining that he was quitting "in protest of excessive secrecy and internal opposition" before ending the letter by asking the administration, "Why aren't we spending more time and effort on this issue?" That, of course, is a very good question. But as is usually the case, there are simply far more questions than there are answers.

Further Readings

Here in this section we are going to take a look at some of the great reading material and resources that helped to make this book possible. If you would like to learn more about any particular piece of subject matter covered in this book, you can find additional information in the following resources. Feel free to check them out for yourself.

Daemonic Reality. Patrick Harper
Many complex topics are addressed in this book, such as parallel dimensions, quantum mechanics and the like. If you are at all confused by some of these heady topics of discussion, Patrick Harper's *Daemonic Reality* is an exhaustive resource on just about every single metaphysical subject known to man. Note that in Harper's usage, the word "Daemonic" simply means "alternate" or "other"—he's not talking about demons, he's simply describing other means by which reality can be perceived. This book is a real eye-opener to be sure.

Hunt for the Skin-Walker: Science Confronts the Unexplained at a Remote Ranch in Utah. Colm A Kelleher and George Knapp
Published in 2005, this book is a true classic when it comes to the Skinwalker Ranch. This is the book that first dropped the bombshell story of what was going on in Utah, and it still remains a brilliant piece of investigative journalism on one of the strangest places on Earth. Written with riveting firsthand accounts, it has George Knapp—the same veteran journalist who introduced the world to Area 51 whistleblower Bob Lazar—as a main contributor. Knapp recounts his own experience when he was imbedded with Robert Bigelow's now defunct National Institute of Discovery Science, clearly laying out exactly what he and others experienced. If you would like to get a few extra

details as to what transpired in this haunted corner of Utah during the late 1990s and early 2000s, this book is your go-to source.

Path of the Skin-Walker. Ryan Skinner

Ryan Skinner—the guy with the perfect name to be talking about skin-walkers—spins us up a real tale in this piece. From the outset, the disclaimer has to be made that this book is entirely subjective. There is no real evidence that any of it transpired except for Ryan's own testimony. Of course, this can be said of many paranormal tales, but George Knapp's reporting in *Hunt for the Skin-Walker* is arguably much more authoritative.

While Knapp met with and interviewed most of the key people involved with Skinwalker Ranch, and actually spent time with the NIDS research crew in an official capacity, Ryan Skinner is an admitted trespasser on the property. But as long as you take his accounts with a grain of salt, the fact that he was an independent and unknown observer during the more legitimate work at the ranch actually provides some invaluable insight that can be used to compare and contrast information from both camps.

Skinwalker Ranch: The UFO Farm. Ryan Skinner

This book is Ryan Skinner's first, and is considered by many to be his best book on the topic. It details how he was initially exposed to the happenings on Skinwalker Ranch, how he got involved, and how he bypassed NIDS security to get onto the property. Ryan relates some rather startling encounters in this book, including the appearance of a traditional Native American skin-walker—upright-walking wolf-body and all—out of a "nebulous mist" that appeared right in front of him.

The Utah UFO Display: A Scientist Brings Reason and Logic to Over 400 UFO Sightings. **Junior Hicks**
Written in the 1970s, this classic book predates all the mainstream literature on the topic. It doesn't mention the Skinwalker Ranch by name (at that time it was owned by the Myers family) but it does detail plenty of strange and anomalous activity in and around that particular section of Utah. If you would like more of a background on the region and past accounts of the unexplained occurrences there, this book is a good resource.

Monsters Among us: An Exploration of Otherworldly Bigfoots, Wolfmen, Portals, Phantoms, and Odd Phenomena. **Linda S. Godfrey**
This book, although not specifically about the Skinwalker Ranch, mentions the strange happenings in Utah in its exploration of similar events happening in many other places around the world. It is especially interesting to note the similarity of tales of interdimensional doorways or portals opening up over random regions of countryside in much the same way they are alleged to have done over Skinwalker Ranch. This book tackles some rather complex and strange events, and as such serves as a great cross reference for the phenomena of Skinwalker Ranch.

www.nbcnews.com
In this era of so-called "fake news", NBC has taken a little heat recently, but don't let that deter you from using its website as a resource when it comes to the Skinwalker Ranch! This news site has a plethora of wide-ranging reports spanning many years, as well as in-depth information and interviews with key players such as Robert Bigelow, NIDS scientists, and even figures involved with the recent Pentagon UFO disclosure regarding Bigelow Aerospace. If you would like to look at the nuts and bolts of how the story of Skinwalker Ranch was built, this where NBC really delivers!

Also by Conrad Bauer

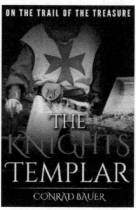
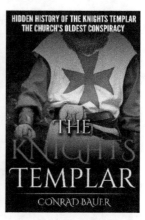

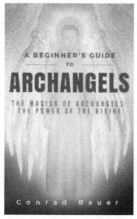
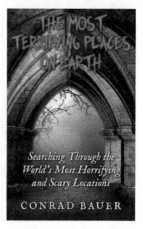

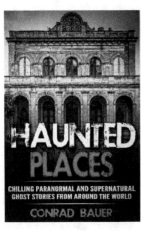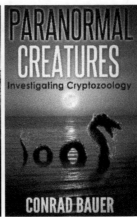

Printed in the USA
CPSIA information can be obtained
at www.ICGtesting.com
LVHW010056200624
783543LV00006B/309